MW00994847

MBER ONE

VINTAGE

EMBLEMS

LOGO DESIGN

SYMBOLS

INSPIRATION COMPENDIUM

AN IMAGE ARCHIVE FOR
ARTISTS and DESIGNERS

EDITIONS
Vault

INTRODUCTION

Are you looking for an inspirational resource for a vintage logo design?

This pictorial archive from Vault Editions is a treasury of 453 engravings and etchings documenting European and British emblems, symbols, insignias, heraldry and coats of arms of the 19th, 18th and 17th-century. Expect to find epic imagery of snakes, skulls, swords, eagles, dragons, serpents, anchors, globes, hammers, lions and the all-seeing eye. Also featured are ornamental banners and scrolls, as well as borders and shields. Highlighted in this collection are also peculiar and rare European emblems such as blindfolded horses, deer with arrows for antlers, swords ablaze with flames and much more.

VINTAGE LOGO DESIGN INSPIRATION

VAULT EDITIONS

FEATURES

This book comes with a unique download link providing instant access to high-resolution files of all images featured. These images can be used in art and graphic design projects or printed and framed to make stunning decorative artworks.

DOWNLOAD YOUR FILES

Downloading your files is simple. To access your digital files, please go to the last page of this book and follow the instructions.

For technical assistance, please email:
info@vaulteditions.com

Bibliographical Note

This book is a new work created by Vault Editions Ltd.

ISBN: 978-1-925968-54-5

01

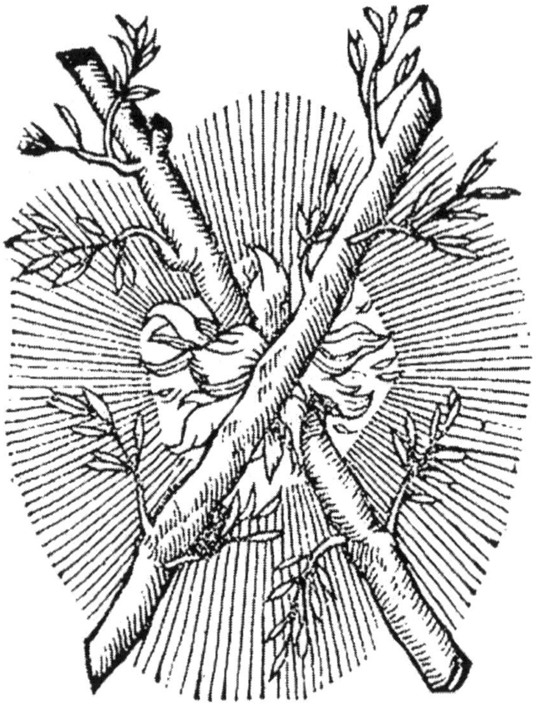

02

03

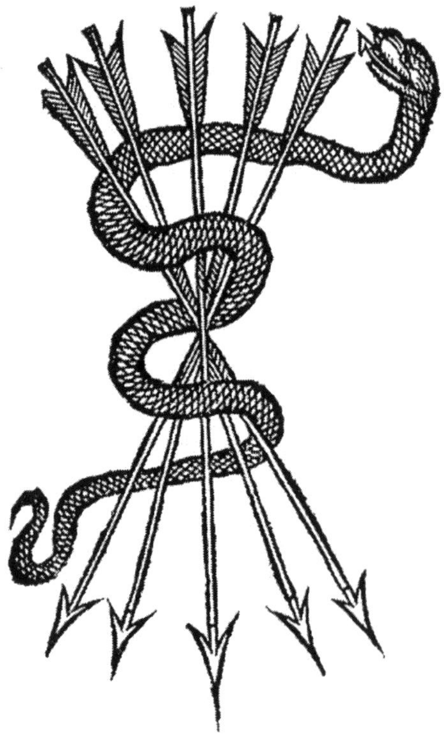

04

05

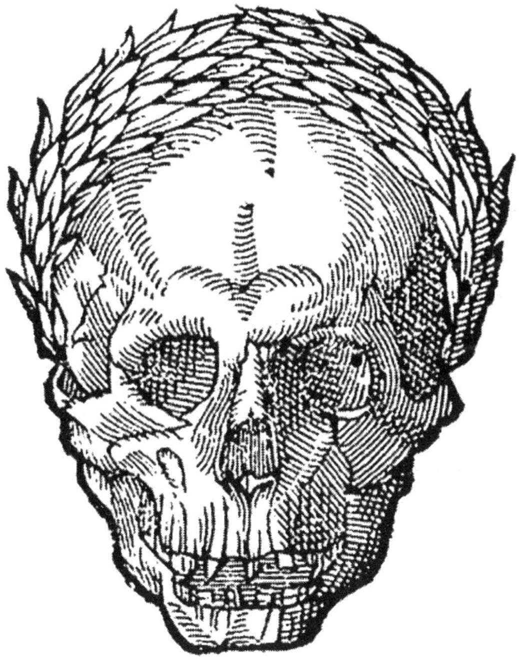

06

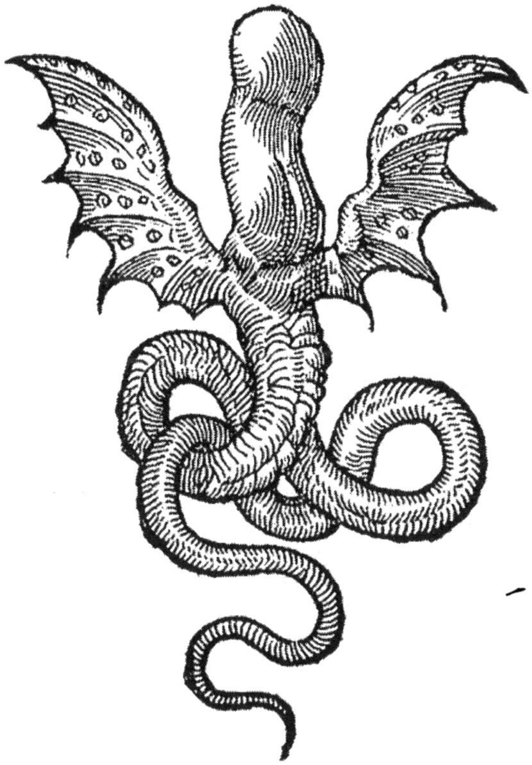

07

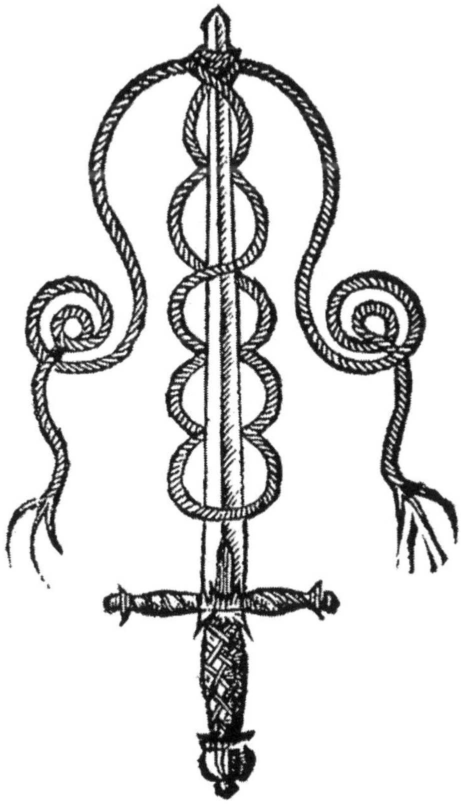

08

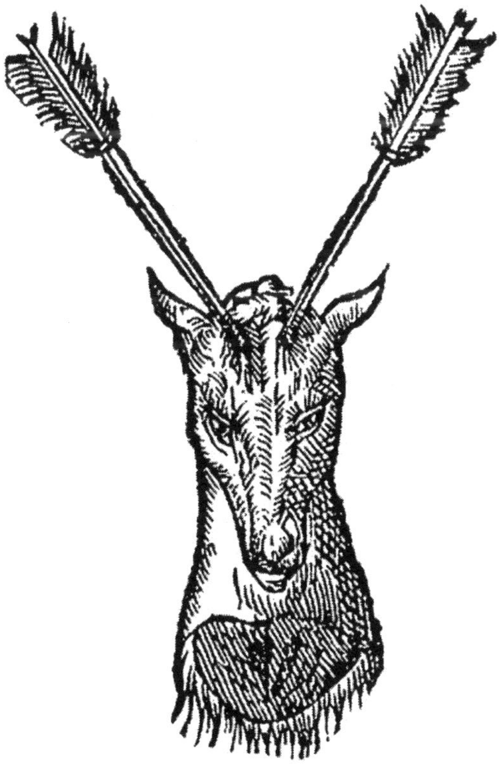

09

10

11

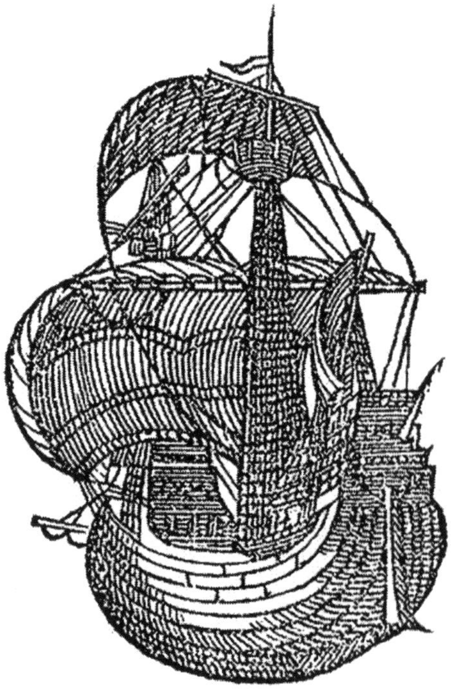

12

13

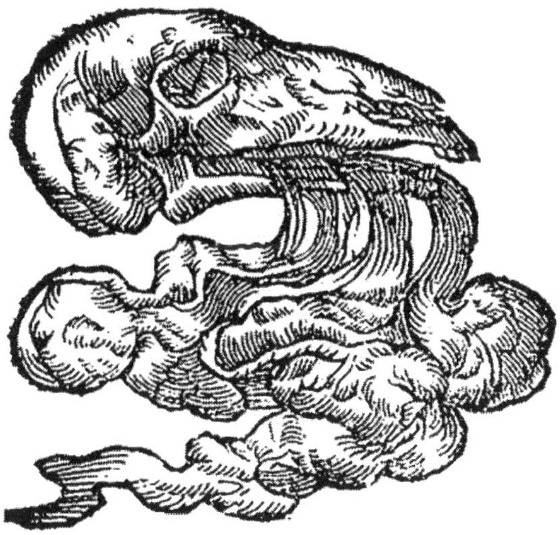

14

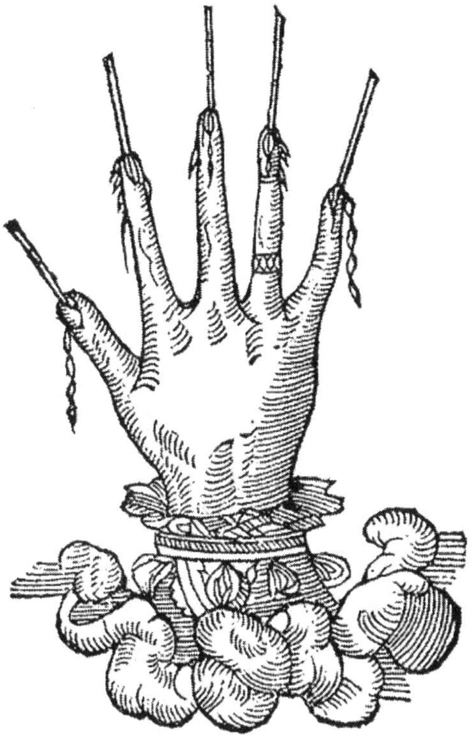

15

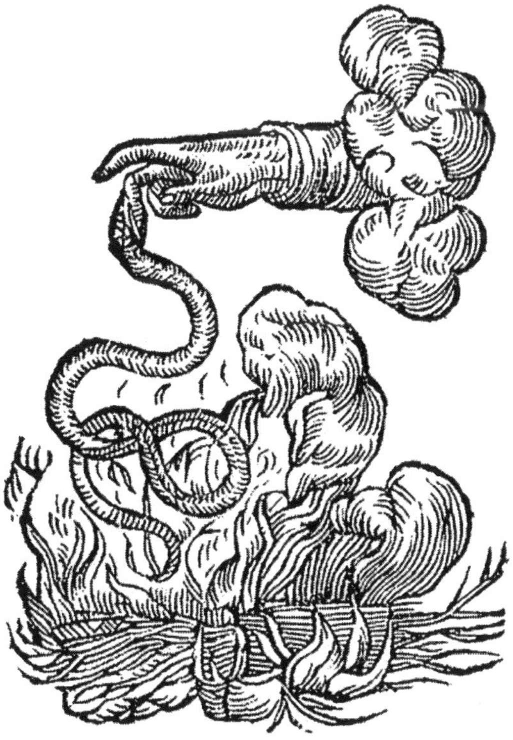

16

17

18

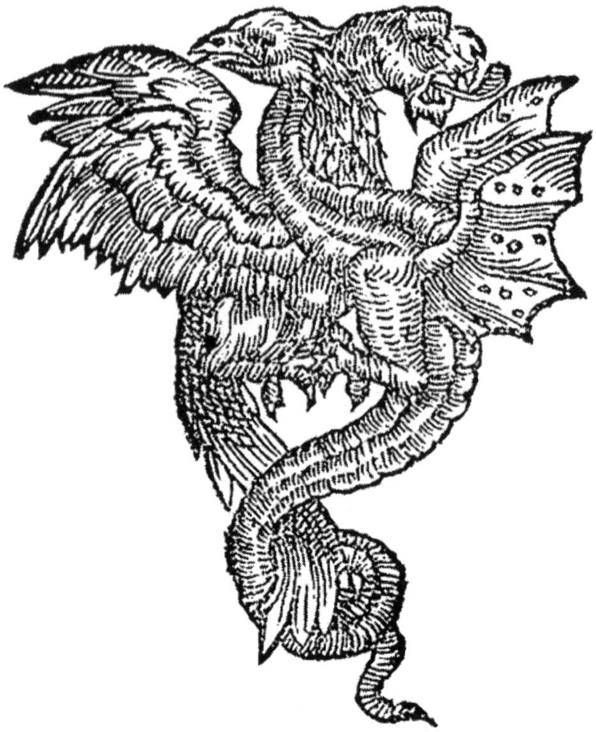

19

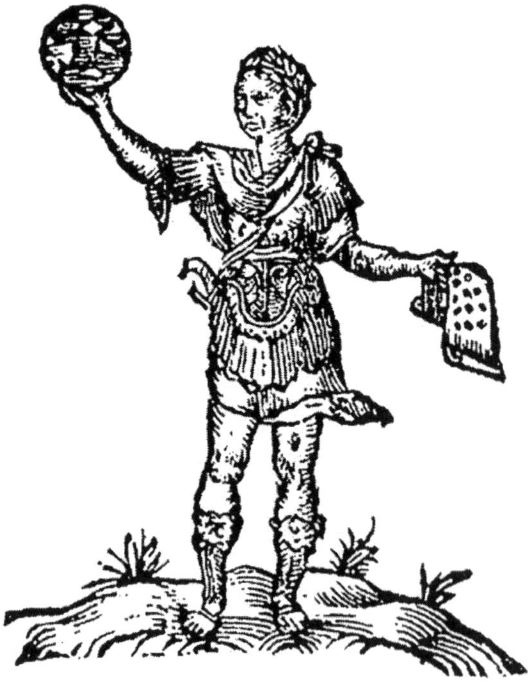

20

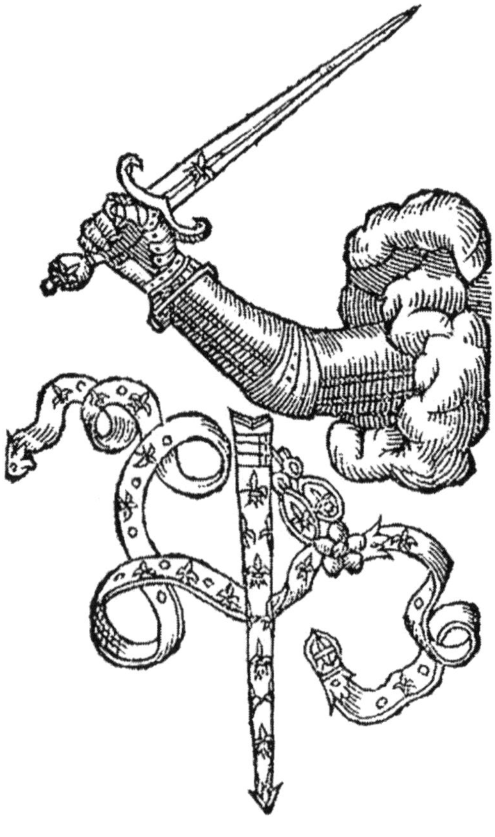

21

22

23

24

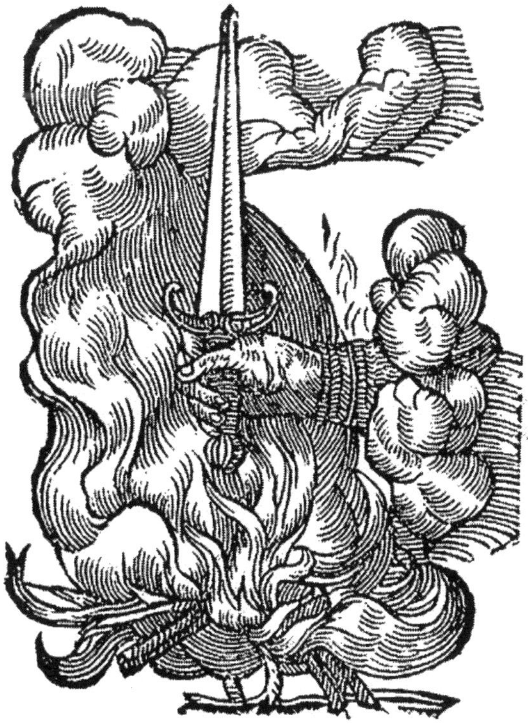

25

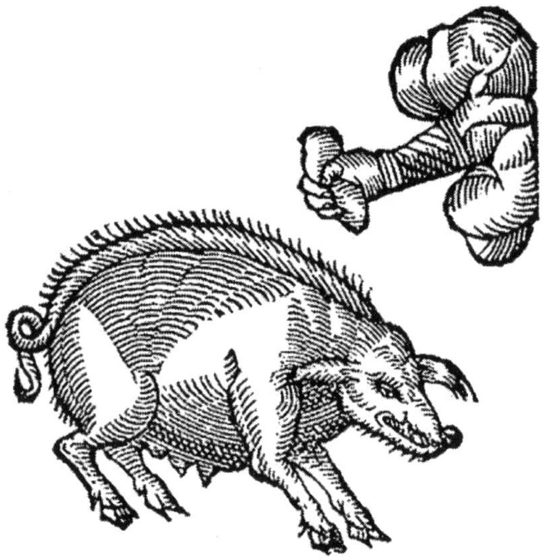

26

27

28

29

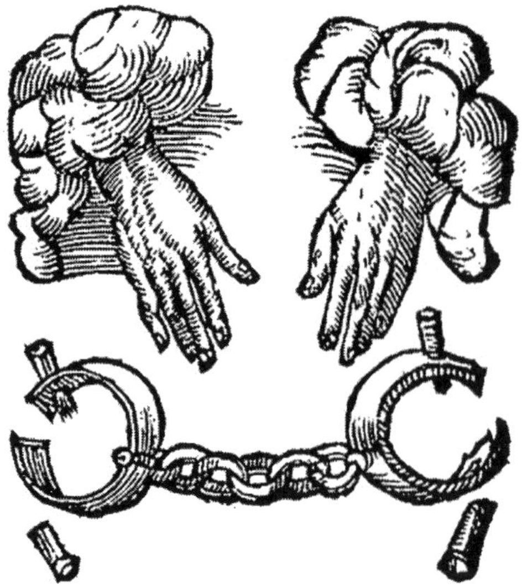

30

31

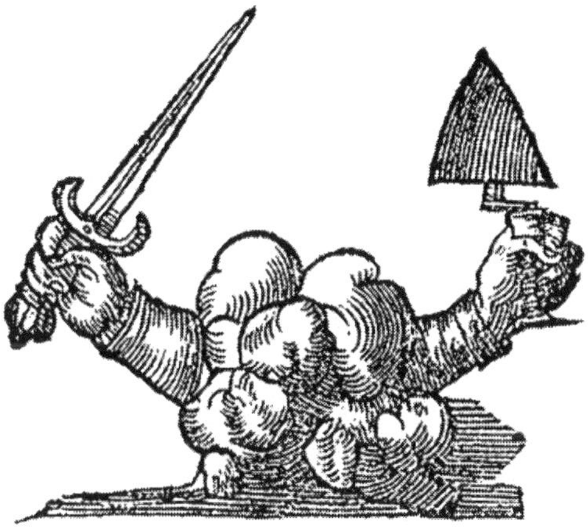

32

33

34

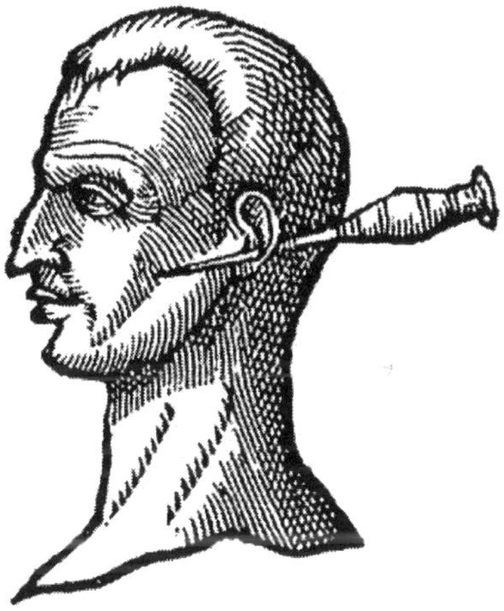

35

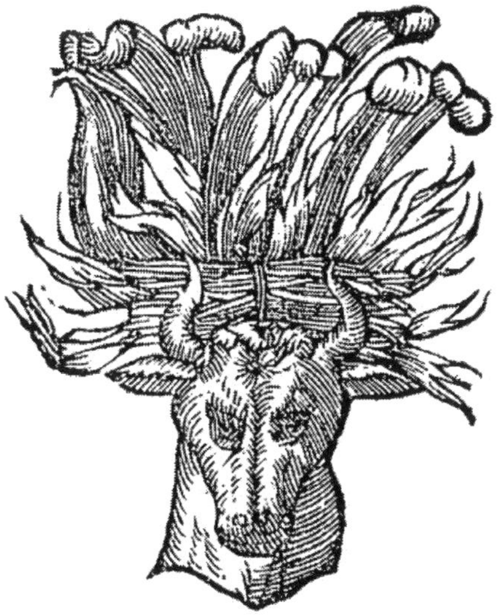

36

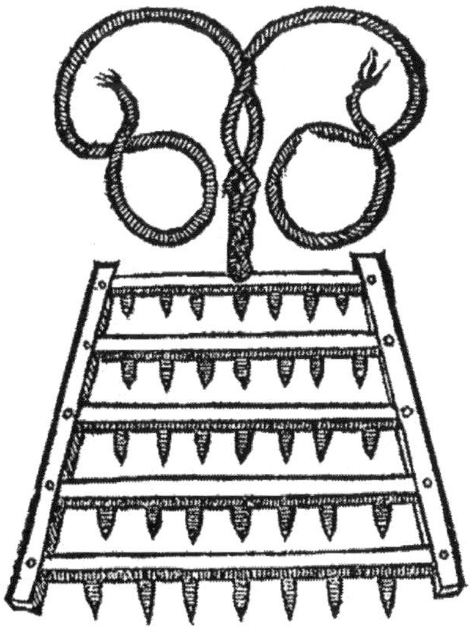

37

38

39

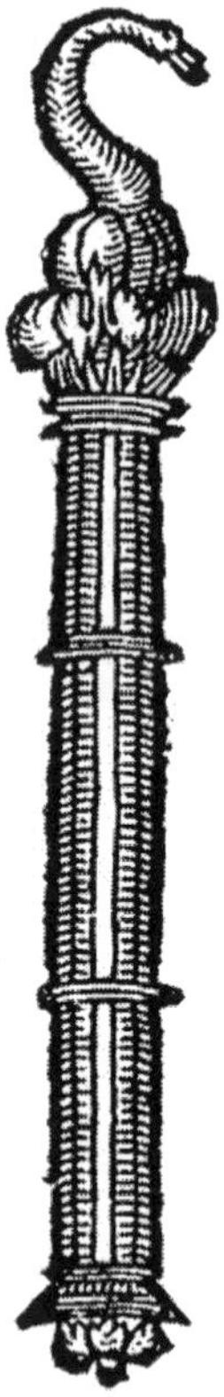

40

41

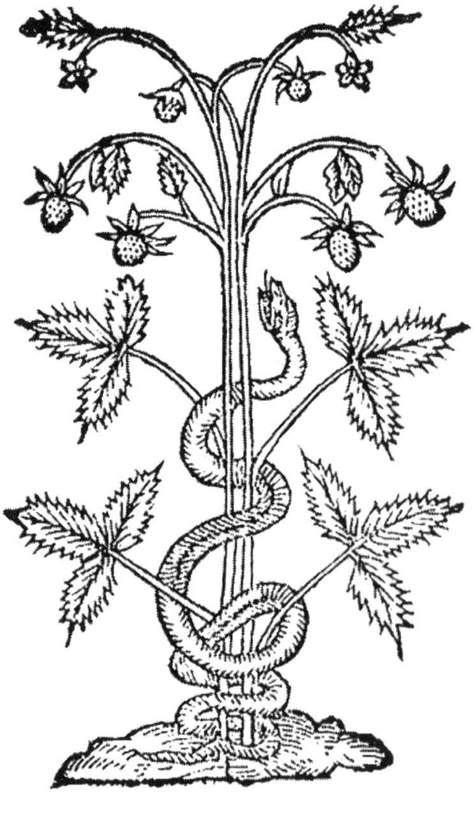

42

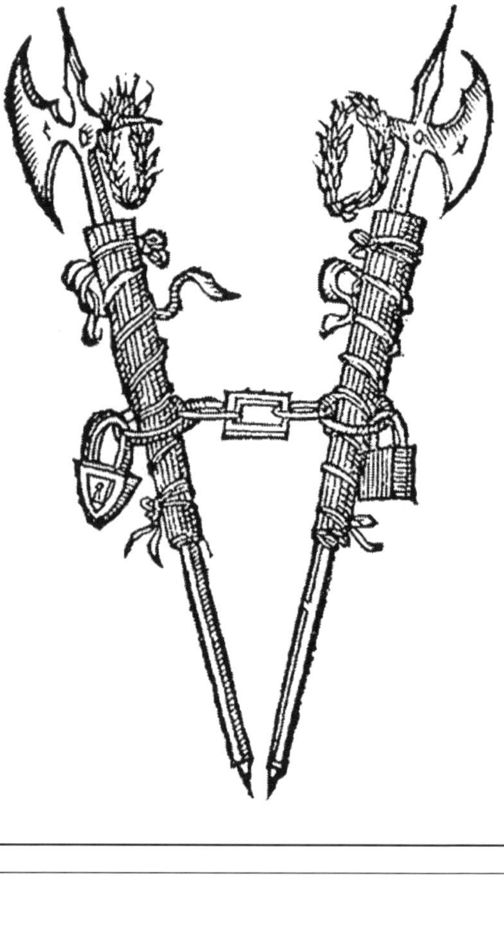

43

44

45

46

47

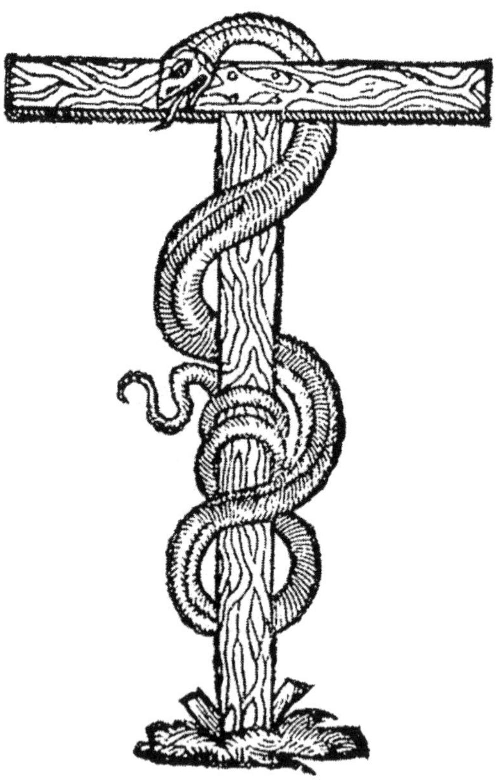

48

49

50

51

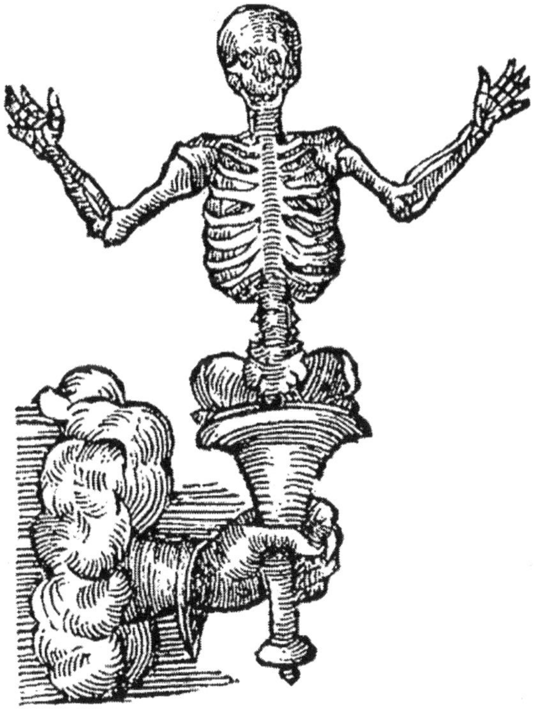

52

53

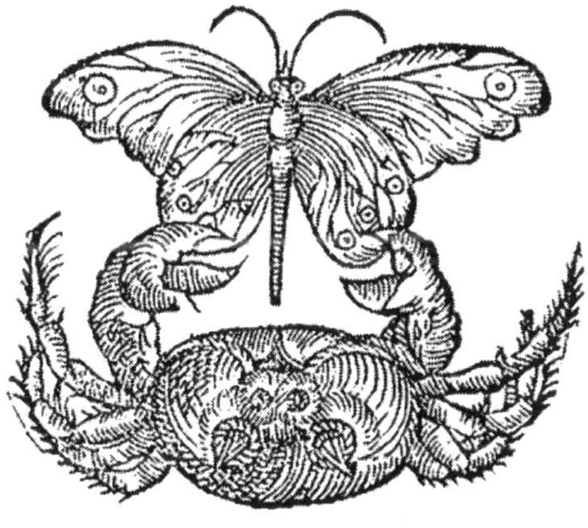

54

55

56

57

58

59

60

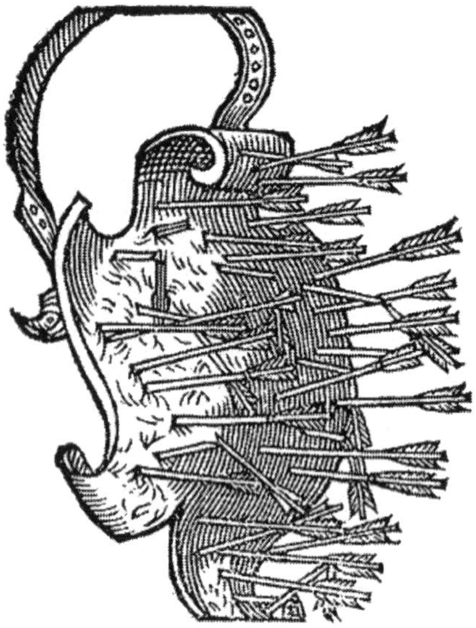

61

62

63

64

65

66

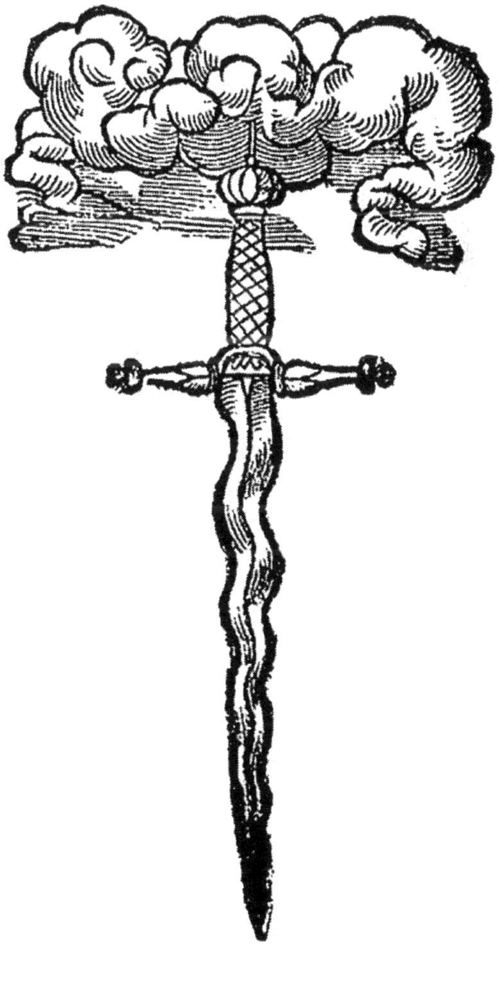

67

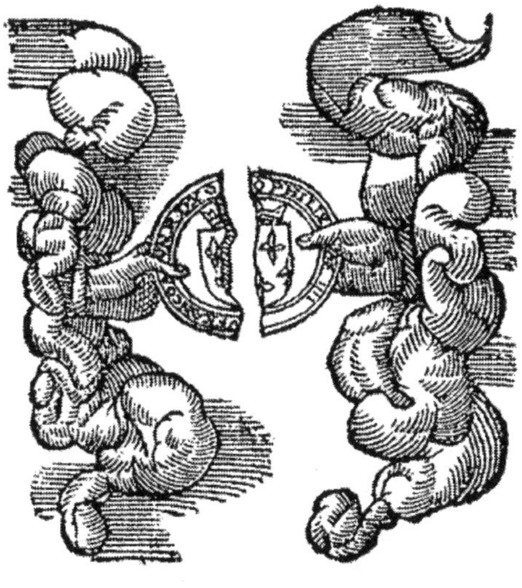

68

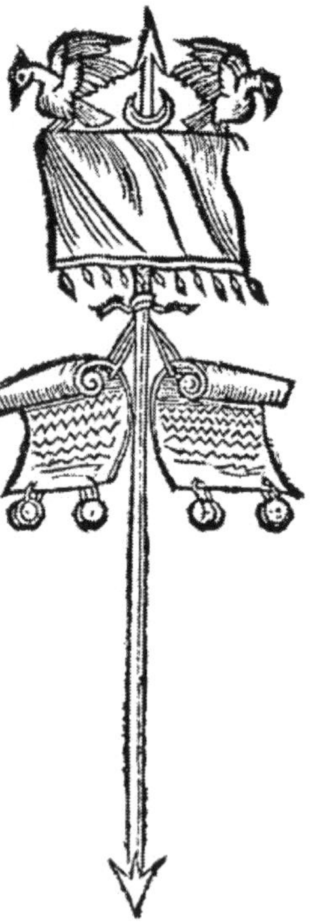

69

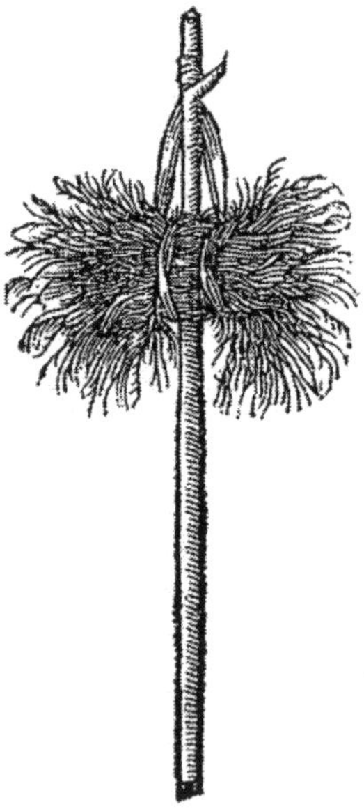

70

71

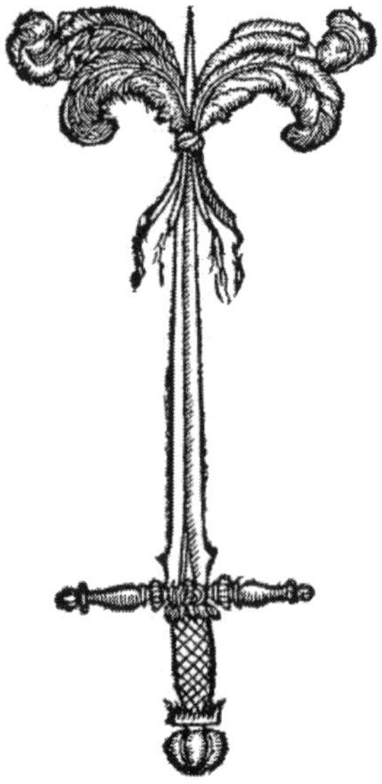

72

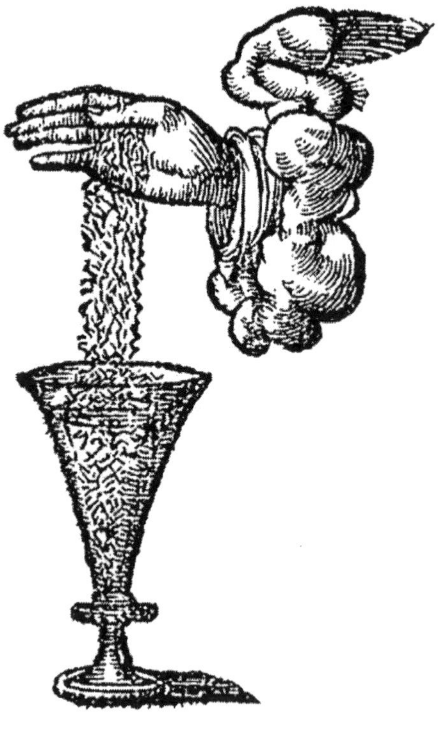

73

74

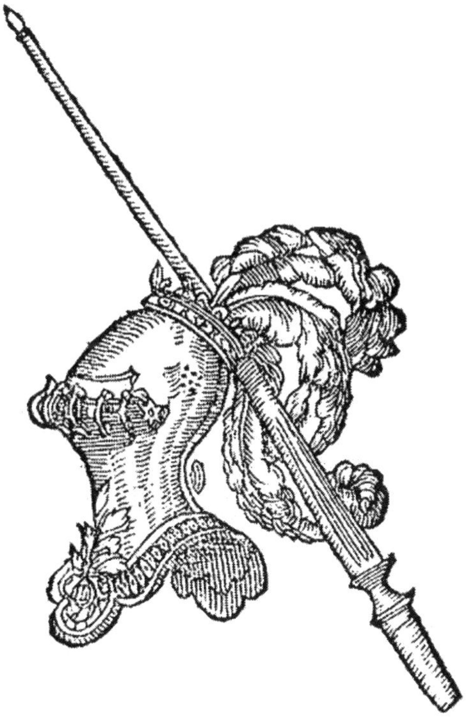

75

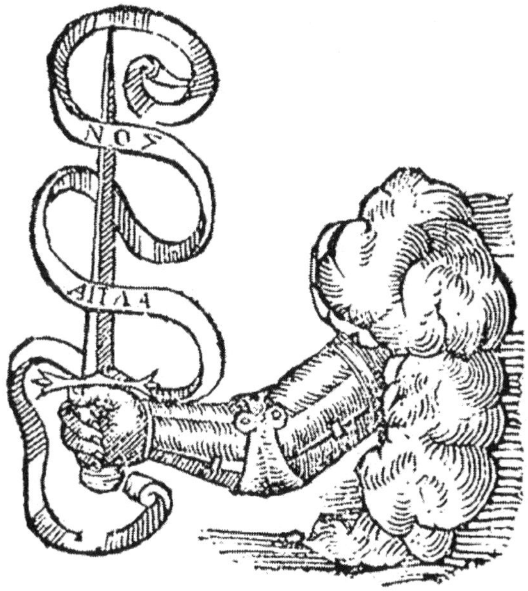

76

77

78

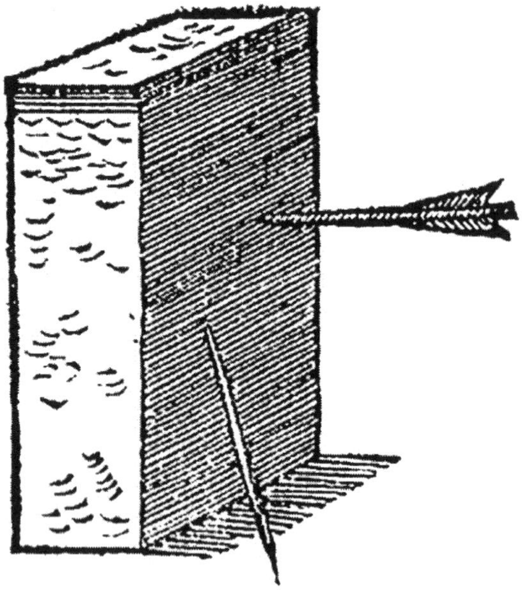

79

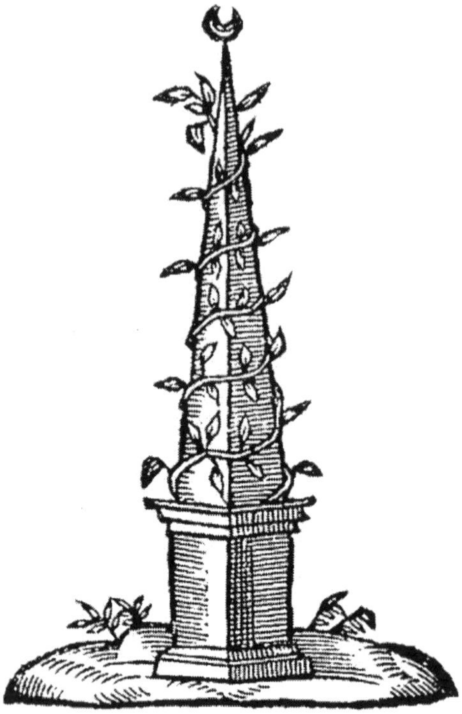

80

83

81

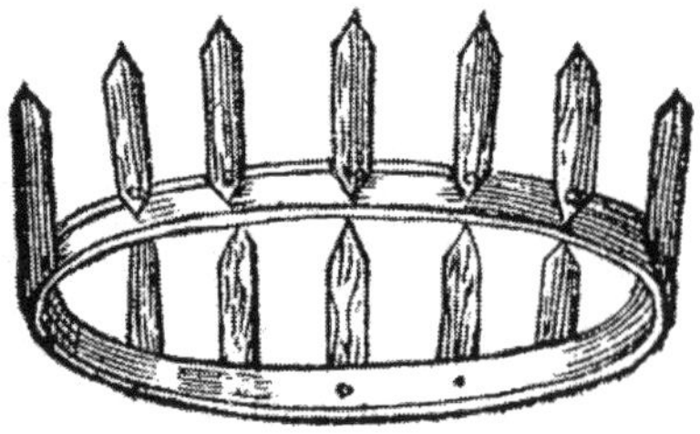

82

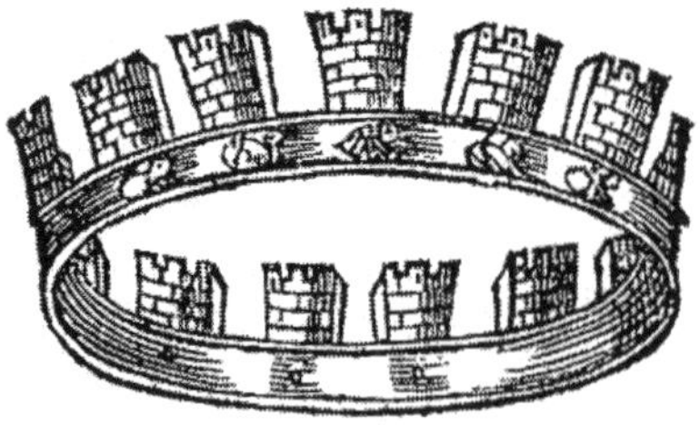

84

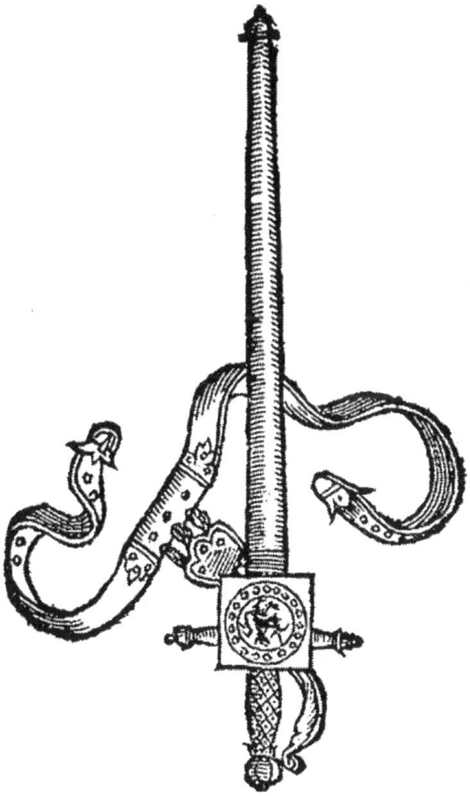

85

86

87

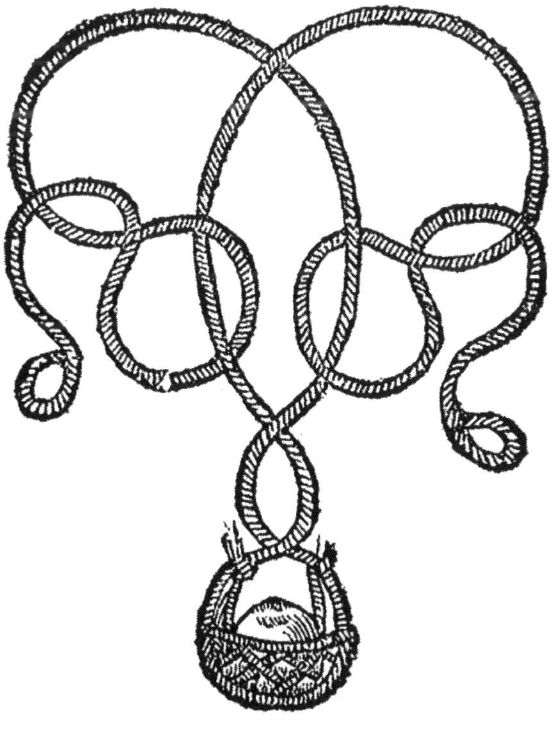

88

89

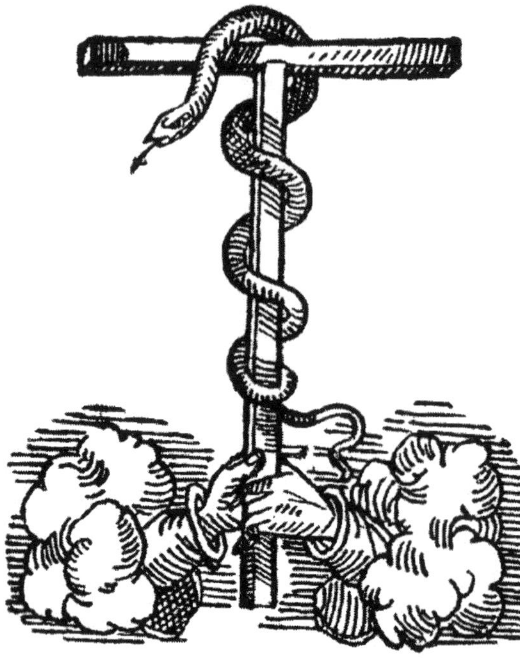

90

91

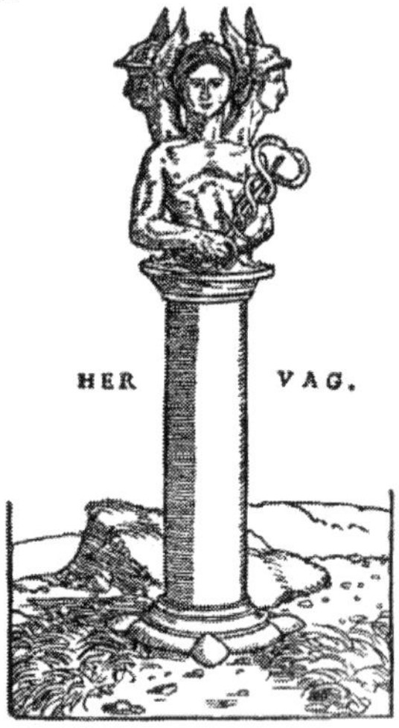
HER
VAG.

92

93

94

MOVRIR ET
DVRER
NON PERIR.

95

MORI ET NON
DVRARE,
PERIRE.

96

SOLA
TEM PVS
HANC ACIEM
RETVNDIT VIRTVS.

97

QVIS CONTRA NOS.
SI DEVS PRO NOBIS

98

I C

99

AL DVS.

100

SCRVTA MINI.

101

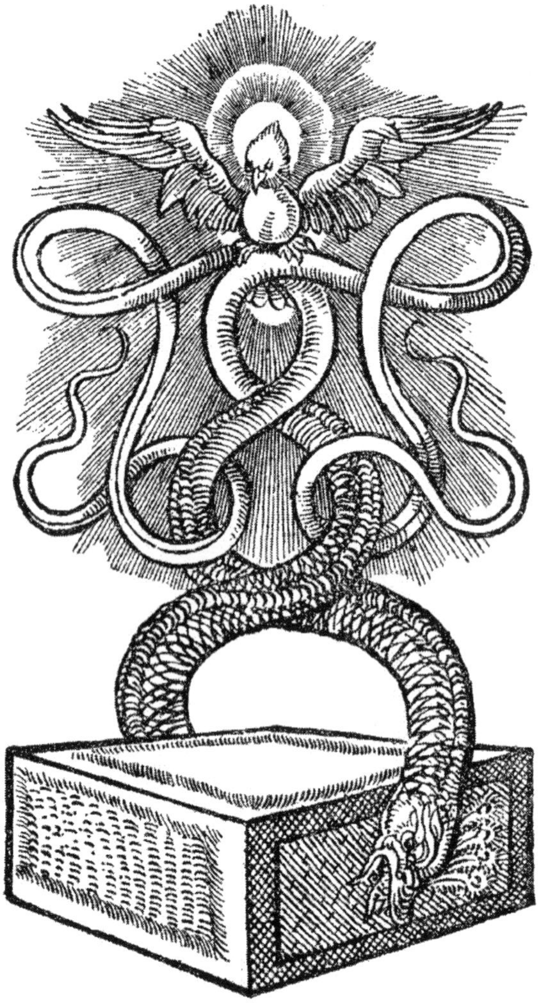

102

SIC VIRTVS OP-
PRESSA RESVRGIT.
G D
L N

103

OMNIBVS, SED
PAVCIS LVCEO.

104

SCIENTIA
IMMVTA
BILIS.

105

OMNIBVS · SED · PAVCIS · LVCEO ·

106

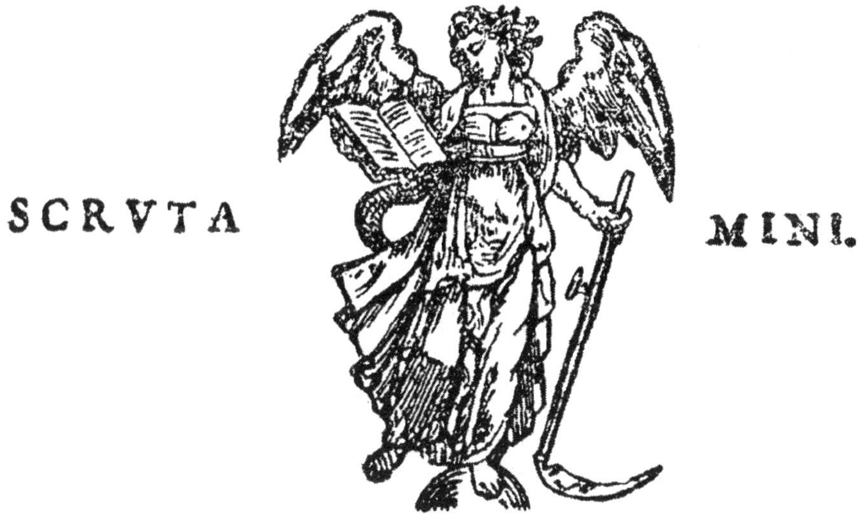
SCRVTA
MINI.

107

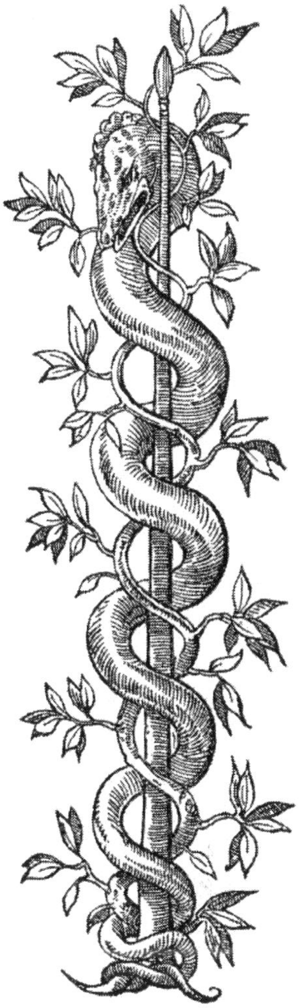

108

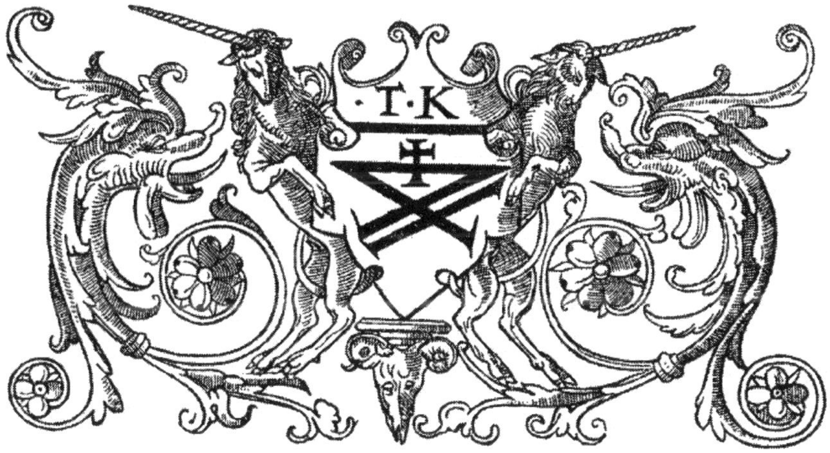
·T·K

109

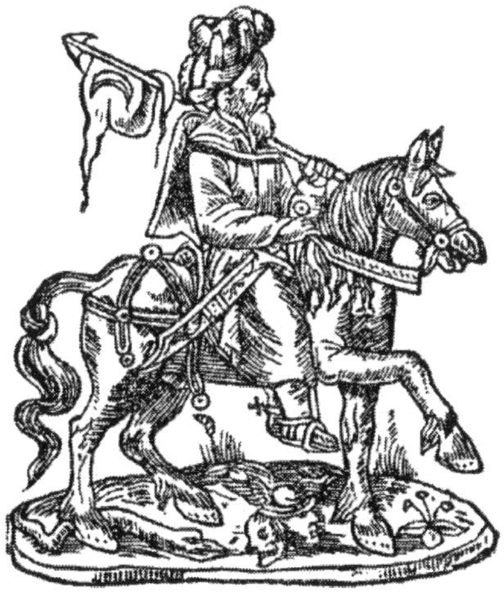

110

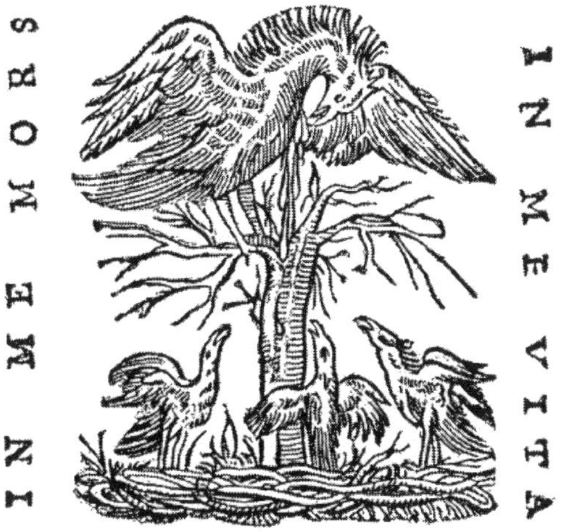
IN ME MORS
IN ME VITA

111

112

113

114

115

116

EXCRVCECOR·

117

VNIVERSITAS RERVM, VT
PVLVIS, IN MANV IEHOVAE.

118

ASSEZ VA QVI
FORTVNE PASSE.

119

MENS NON TER
PROVIDA RITE

120

SCABRA DOLO

121

IN VIRTVTE
ET FORTVNA.

122

OMNI TEMPORE DILI-
GIT, QVI AMICVS EST.
PROVERBIORVM XVII
AMICITIAM DISTANTIA LOCI NON SEPARAT

123

OMNIA
LABOR
VINCIT
IMPROBVS.

124

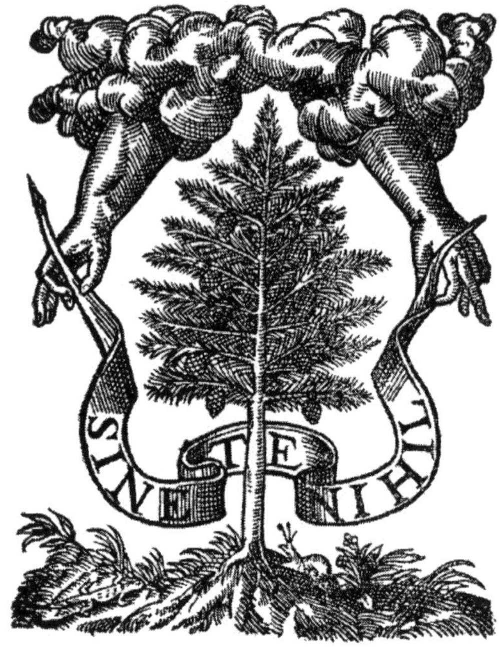
SINE TE NIHIL

125

SPES MEA CHRIST
ANTONIVS BERTRAM ANNO M D LXXXIIII

126

VIRTVTE ET
CONSTANTIA.

127

VIN
CEN
TI

128

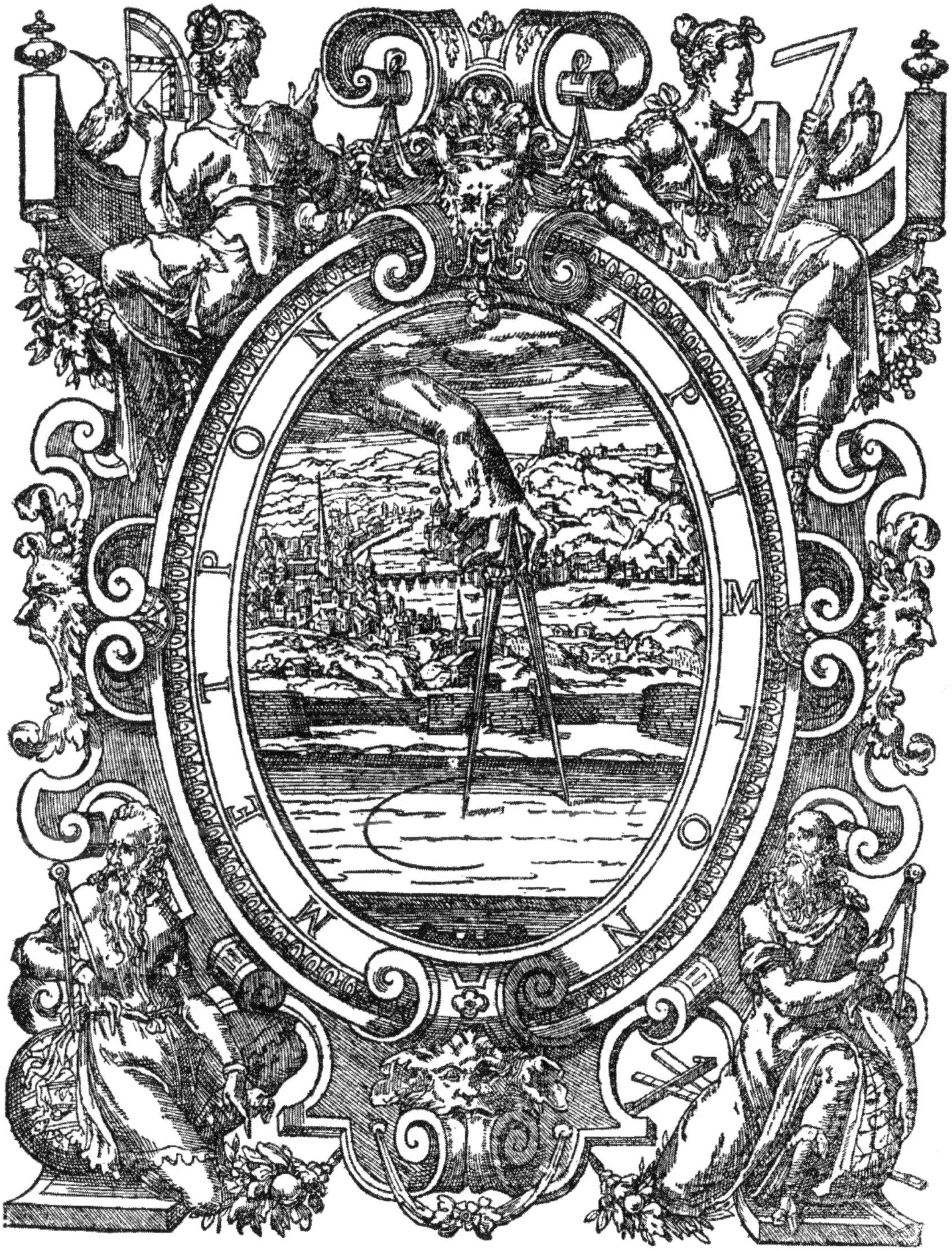

129

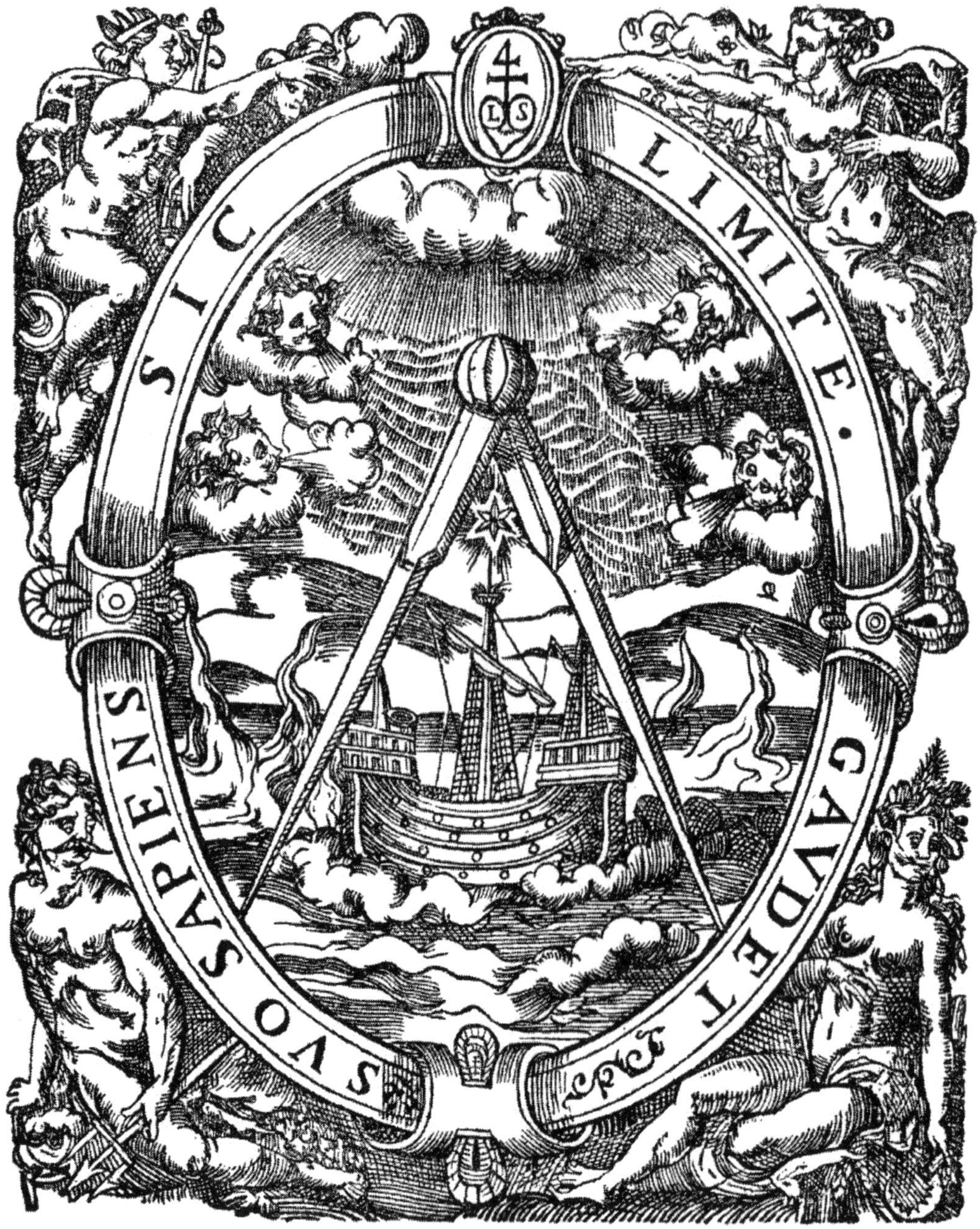
SIC LIMITE.
GAVDET
SVO SAPIENS
L S

130

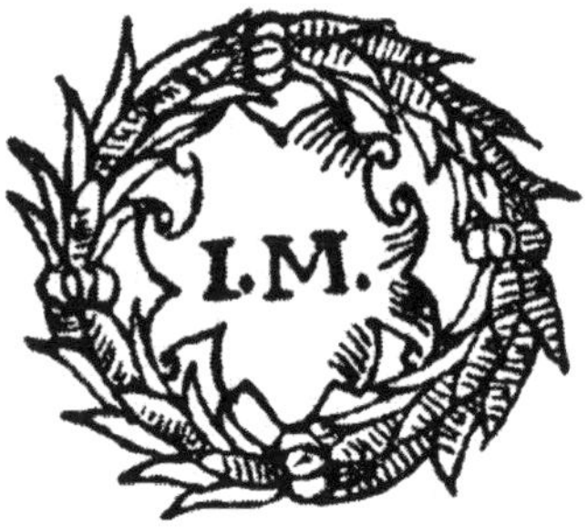
I.M.

131

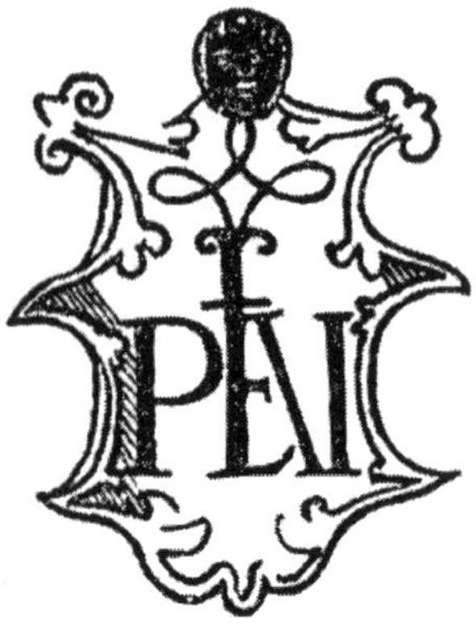

132

133

CONCORDIA RES PARVÆ CRESCVNT, DISCORDIA MAXIMÆ DILABVNTVR
MANIBVS
CONTRAHITVR, CONSERVATVR
CORDE
SOCIETAS
VERBIS INITVR,

134

135

136

137

138

139

140

141

142

FRVCTVS PAVLATIM
FLORI
SVCCRESCIT

143

144

ΠΟΝΟΥ
ΑΝΕΥ ΠΕΝΙΑ

145

VITIS
VERA
CHRISTV

146

147

DEI. AD SALVTEM
OMNI CREDENTI.
POTENTIA SIQVIDEM EST
VITÆ AD VITAM
MORTIS AD MORTEM
Ad Rho. I.
Ecce, positus est hic in ruinam, & in resurrectionem
multorum in Israël, & in signum cui contradicitur.

148

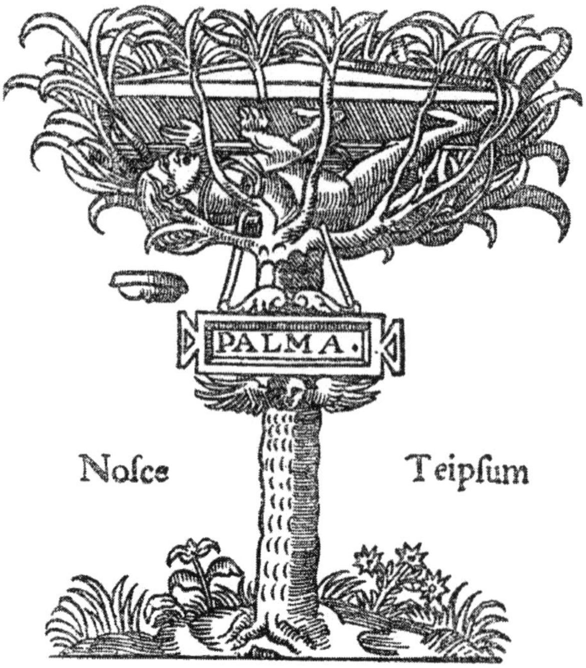
PALMA.
Nosce
Teipsum

149

PACEM.
VICTIS,
N,
BOVCHER

150

ΠΑΝ
ΔΕΝΔΡΟΝ
ΑΓΑΘΟΝ
ΚΑΡΠΟΥΣ
ΚΑΛΟΥΣ
ΠΟΙΕΙ

151

Alteri seruiens cõsumor

152

Alteri seruiens consumor.

153

SCOPVS VITÆ MEA.
CHRIST

154

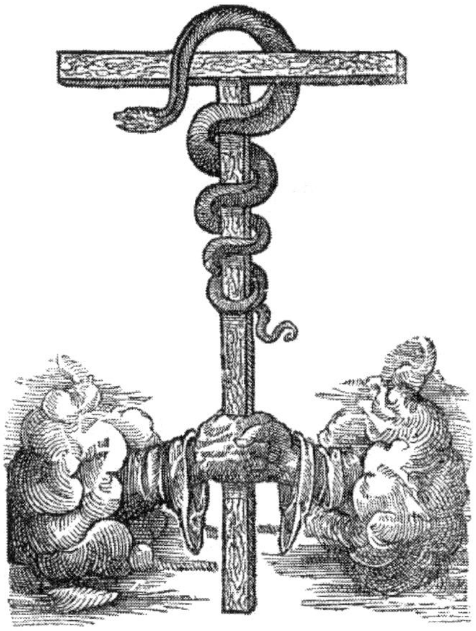

155

PRINCIPIVM EX FIDE,
FINIS IN CHARITATE.

156

PRINCIPIVM EX FIDE,
FINIS IN CHARITATE.

157

Almus ineſt ardor,
flammam experies terendo.

158

IN VTRVNQVE
PARATVS

159

160

161

162

163

164

165

166

167

168

169

170

171

172

173

VINCENTINO
VICTOGLORIA

174

MATT, XI

175

SCOPVS VITAE MEAE CHRISTVS

176

177

VNDIQVE PRÆCIPITIVM
D B G

178

SIC VT
RESCIT·IVSTVS

179

SACRÆ CONCORDIÆ PRVDENTIA COMES

180

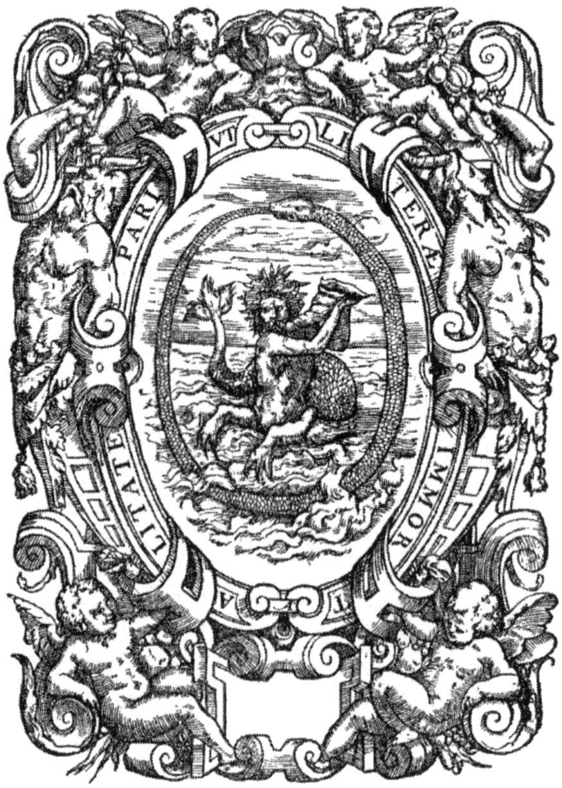

181

I
H

182

NIL·DEVS·HAC·NOBIS·MAIVS·CONCESSIT·IN·VSVS
TYPVS AMICITIÆ

183

SPES MEA IN DEO EST PSAL. 61

184

OCCASIO TEMPORE·EX OPPORTVNO NASCITVR

185

186

187

188

189

190

191

192

193

194

195

196

197

ADVERSVS EAM
NON PRAEVALEBVNT
ARMA IMPIORVM.

198

NONDVM SATIS PERSPECTA
VIRTVTE FORTVNA ADVERSA

199

200

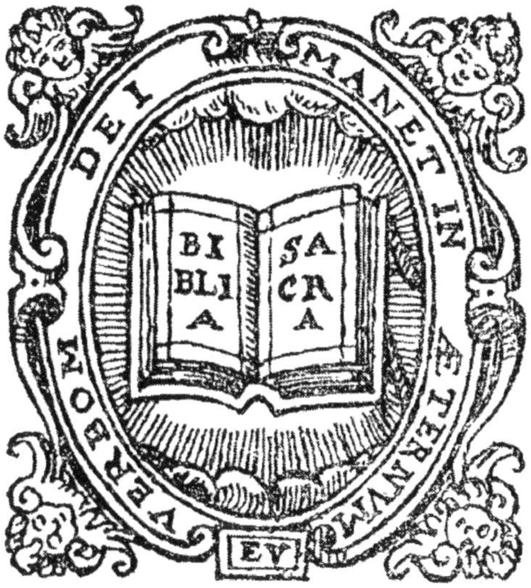

201

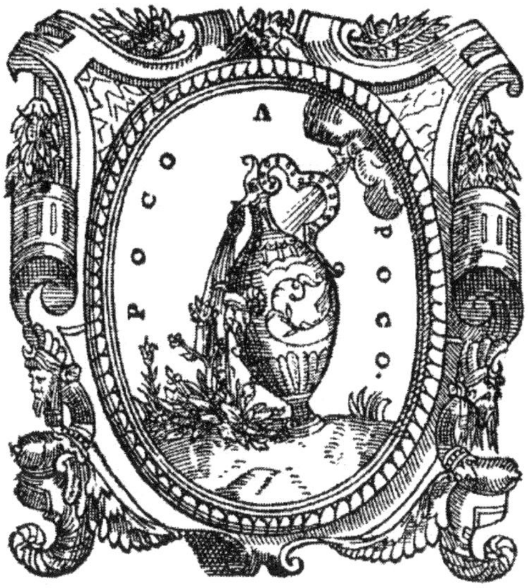

202

203

204

205

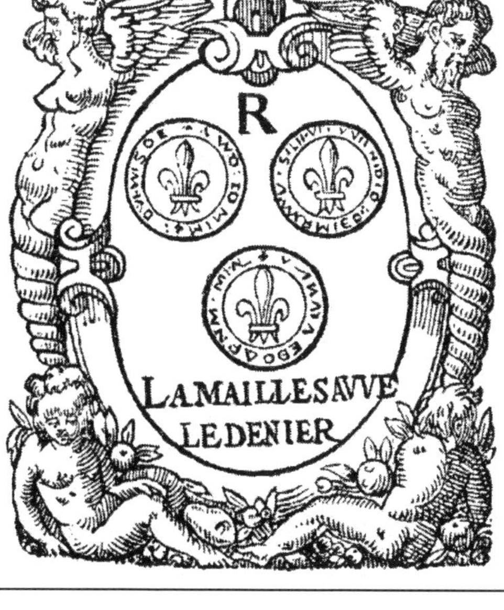

206

207

208

209

210

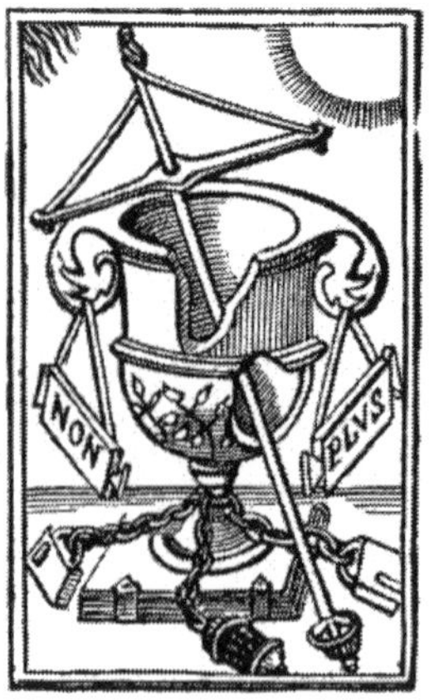

211

212

213

214

RI
PIERRE:RICOVART

215

Fecitq3deus duo luminaria magna.gene.i.
Tibi dabo claues regni celorum.math.xvi.
Vas electionis est michi iste.actu.ix.
RI
PIERRE:RICOART
Sainct Pierre & sainct Pol.

216

META LABORIS HONOR

217

218

219

220

221

222

223

224

225

226

227

228

I C

229

QVOD TIBI
FIERI NON
VIS, ALTERI
NE FECERIS.

230

QVOD TIBI
FIERI NON
VIS. ALTERI
NE FECERIS.

231

*QVAERE,
NEC
VLTRA

232

QVOD TIBI FI
ERI NON VIS,
ALTERI NE
FECERIS.
VI
VII
RVM
CCL
DE
RI
MIL
PE
LE
RE
NVM

233

234

235

236

237

238

239

240

241

242

243

244

TOLLIT AD
ASTRA VIRTVS

245

CVTE
ALBVS
INTVS

246

PARTOVT AMOVR
TOVT PAR AMOVR
AMOVR PAR TOVT
EN TOVT BIEN
AMOR DEI
DENIS IANOT

247

·FORTVNA·
AVDACES·
·IVVAT·
LH
·LAVRENS·HYLLAIRE·

248

249

250

251

252

253

254

255

256

257

258

259

260

DVM
SVPEREM
VIC TRIX

261

TEGE.NOS.✝SVB.VM
BRA.
ALARVM.TVA
RVM.PRO

262

263

COL
NEM

264

LITERAE IMMORTALITATEM PARIVNT

265

266

267

SPES NON CONFVNDIT.

268

269

270

271

272

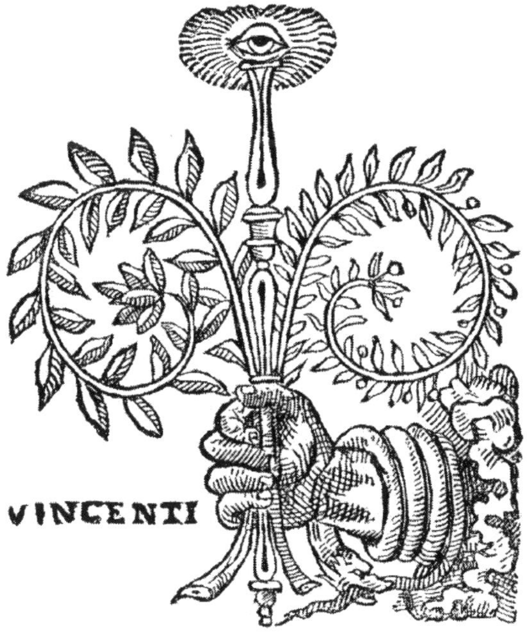

273

274

SOLI DEO HONOR
VIRTVS ET GLORIA.

275

276

fortuna nequit
Inconſtans
quòd ſtare
quieſcit.

277

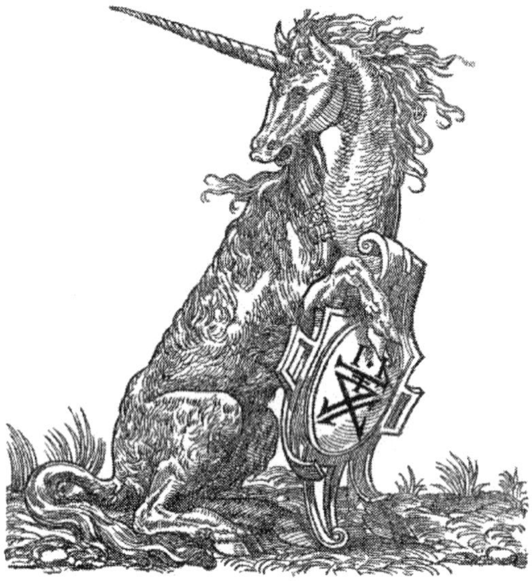

278

Inconſtans fortuna ne-
quit quòd ſtare quieſcit.

279

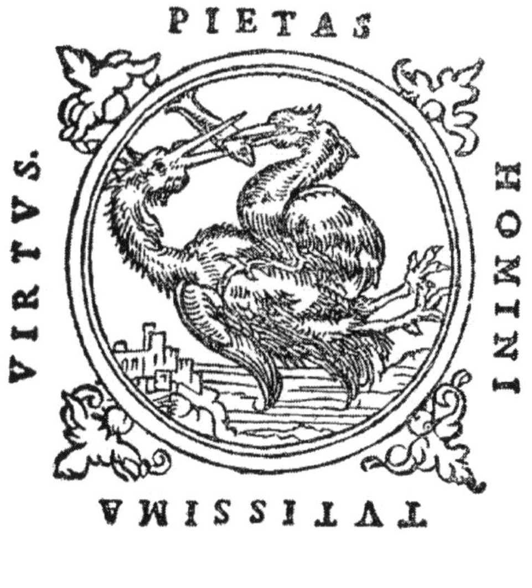
PIETAS
HOMINI
TVTISSIMA
VIRTVS.

280

VIRTVTE DVCE,
COMITE FORTVNA.

281

NON VENI PACEM MITTERE, SED
GLADIVM. MATTH. X.
VENI IGNEM MITTERE. LVC XII.

282

VIRTVTE DVCE,
COMITE FORTVNA.
1540.

283

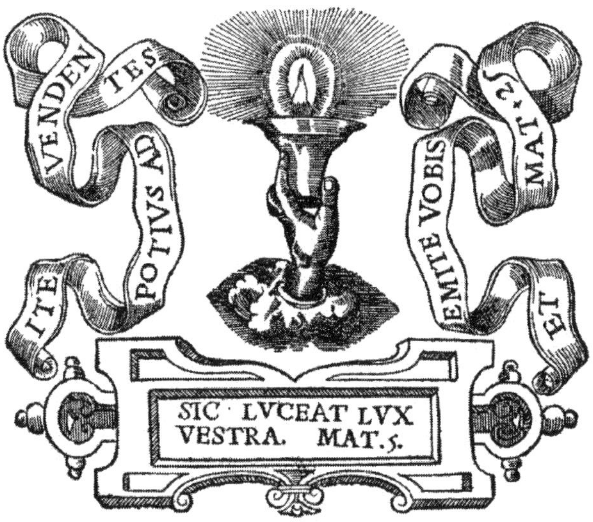
ITE VENDEN TES
POTIVS AD
EMITE VOBIS
ET MAT. 25.
SIC · LVCEAT LVX
VESTRA. MAT. 5.

284

285

286

287

288

289

CORNV COPIA

290

LONGIS
NIHIL IN CARITATE
VIOLENTIA

291

VENIET TEMPVS MESSIONIS

292

SCIENTIAM. COR.
RECTVM INQVIRIT

293

LAVDABILE NOMEN DOMINI &
IHS

294

295

CON STANTIA
LABORE ET

296

297

PER ASPERA VIRTVS AD ASTRA

298

SCIENTIA
IMMVTA
BILIS.

299

300

O
P

301

ALTVM SAPERE SED
NOLI

302

RAMI VT EGO INSERERER
DEFRACTI SVNT

303

IVVENES ET VIRGINES, SENES CVM
IVNIORIBVS LAUDENT NOMEN DOMINI·
ML
I

304

305

Δεύτεραι φροντίδες σοφώτεραι.

306

TOTVM SIC IRRIGAT·ORBEM

307

VICTRICI
GALLIÆ.
G B

308

Iustitia Domini manet in æternum.
RA DOMINI
PEN
DEMVS
OMNES
IN STATE

309

310

311

312

313

314

315

316

317

318

319

320

321

322

323

324

325

326

327

328

329

330

331

STANTE ET CVRRENTE ROTA

332

DV PRE DIEV FAIT SOR-
TIR LE FOING, POVR
LE BESTAIL QVI N'A NVL
SOING.
Pſal. 104.

333

334

SCV
TVM
FLO
RENTIÆ

335

336

Habet & musca splenem.
Et formicæ sua bilis inest.

337

338

339

340

341

342

343

344

345

346

347

348

349

350

351

352

353

354

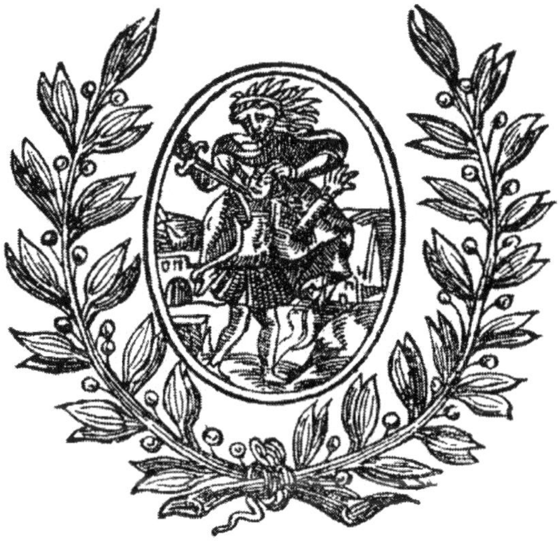

355

CONSTANTIA.
LABORE
ET

356

357

qui arrouse : mais Dieu qui
Celuy qui plante n'est rien, ne celuy
donne accroissement. 1. Corinth. 3.
יהוה

358

359

ADORAMVS.TE.CHRISTE.BENEDITIMVS.TIBI
QVIA.PER.SANTA.CRVSAN.REDEMISTI.MONDON

360

Rame oliue.
Eclefie turris

361

PERIMIT DEXTRA VINCIT LAEVA
A SINISTRA AVETO
OPINIO

362

SACRVM PINGVE DABO·NEC MACRVM SACRIFICABO·

363

PRÆCEPS OCCASIO

364

DVM
SVPEREM
VIC TRIX

365

LAVDABILE NOMEN DOMINI
IHS

366

qui arrouſe : mais Dieu qui
Celuy qui plante n'eſt rien, ne celuy
donne accroiſſement. 1. Corinth. 3.
יְהֹוָה

367

יְהֹוָה

368

CONSTANTIA
ADVERSIS
DVRAT.

369

370

371

372

373

374

375

NON NOBIS DOMINE
NON NOBIS ·SED
NOMINI TVO
DA GLORIAM
NEC BARBAE
NEC BARBATO

376

SCIENTIA
IMMVTA
BILIS.

377

378

379

parquoy tout arbre qui ne fait pas bon
fruit, sera coupé & ietté au feu, Mat. III.
La coignée est ia mise à la racine des arbres:

380

OPERA
ET
NVMIN

381

382

VALLES MADENT
FLVMINE

383

VOTIS
VLTRO
SVCCEDERE

384

PATIENTIA PAVPERIS
NON PERIBIT IN FINEM.

385

META LABO-
RIS HONOR.

386

CONTI-
NET
VIRTVTES
OMNES

387

SCRIPTVRA
DIVINITVS
INSPIRATA
OMNIS
IN CAPI TELIB SCRIP TVM
E ST DE ME PSAL.3

388

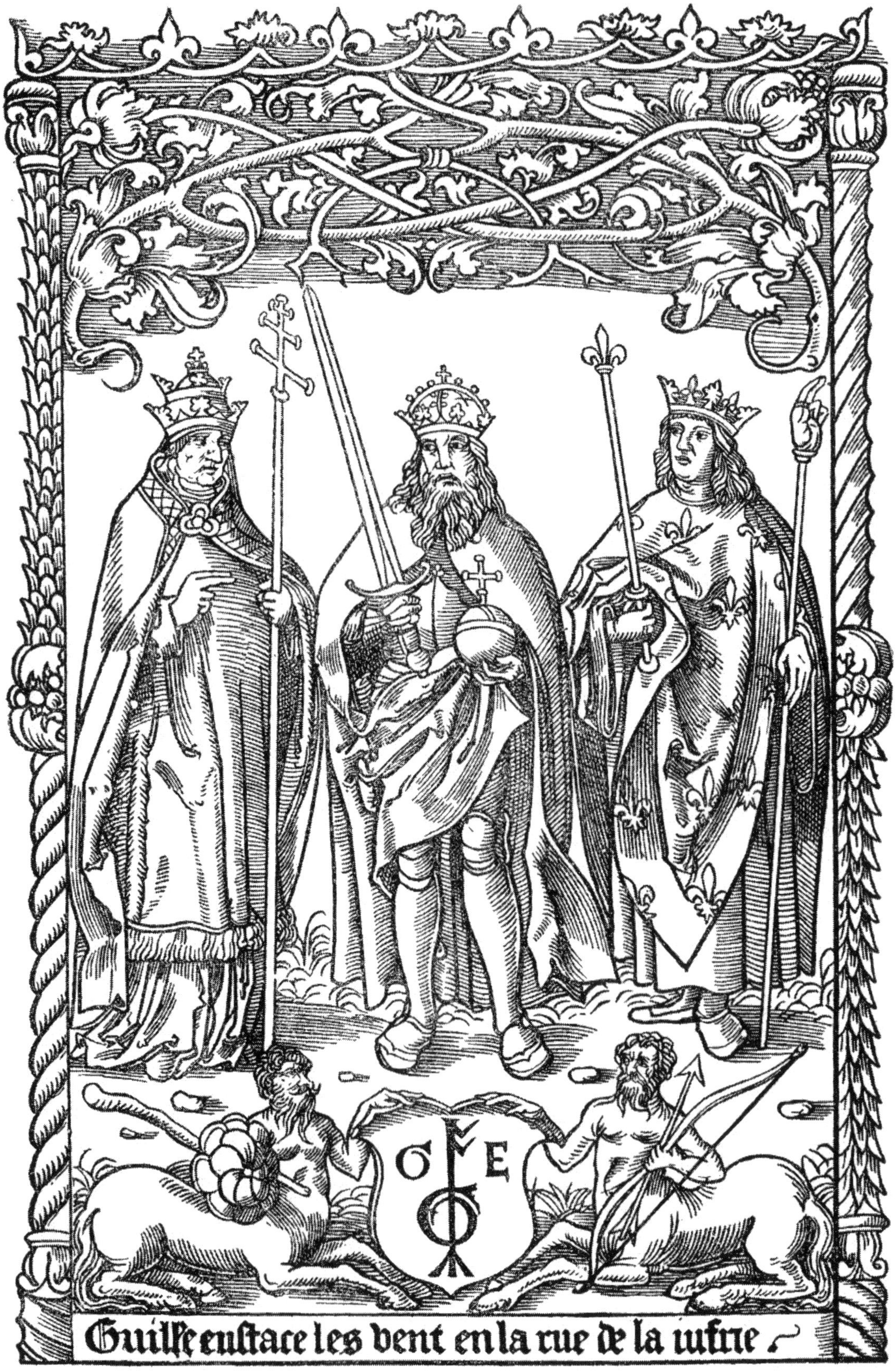
Guille eustace les vent en la rue de la iuifrie

389

390

391

392

393

VINCES IN HOC SIGNO

394

DOMAT INVIDIAM FORTVNA

395

VIRTVS PROSTRATA TEMPORIS INIVRIA

396

MICAT INTER OMNES IVLIVM SIDVS
ARA
CLEMENTIA

397

398

399

400

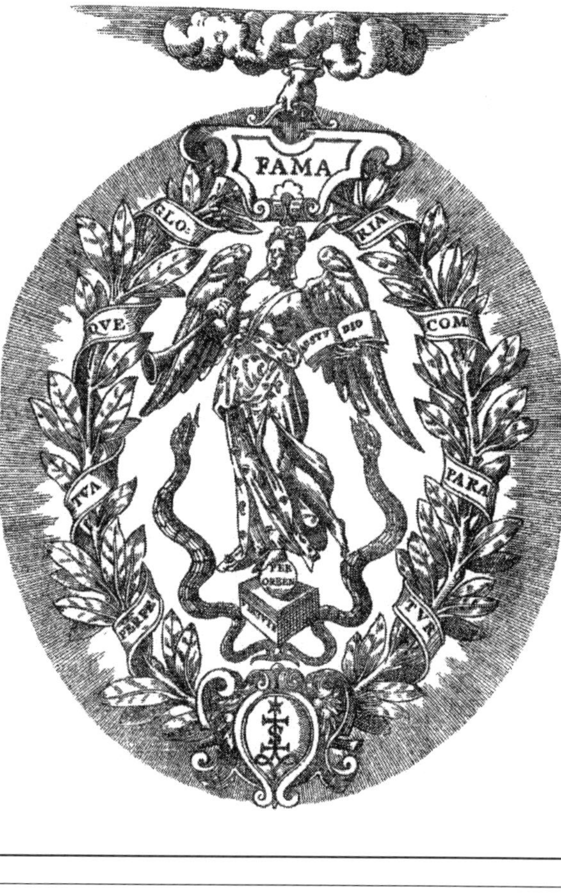

401

402

403

404

405

406

TVM
FLO
RENTIE
SCA

407

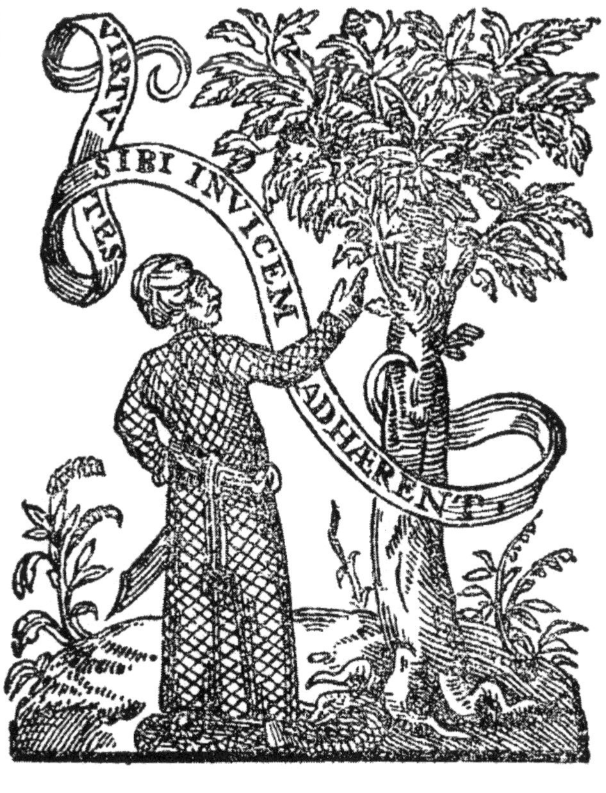
VIRTV
TES
SIBI INVICEM
ADHÆRENT.

408

NOLI
ALTVM SAPERE

409

410

411

412

413

414

415

416

417

ENSEIGNE MOY MON DIEV
QVE TON VOVLOIR IE FACE
TAT QVE AV CELESTE LIEV
IE PVISSE VEOIR TA FACE
P
S.

418

PAVPERES SVSTINE.
FINEM RESPICE.
PRIGENT CALVARIN.
DEVM TIME.
P
C

419

PAR AVIS
IASOM
MEDEE
DENIS ROSSE

420

LE PELLI
CAN
A
G
AMBROISE
GIRAVLT

421

VNICVMAR

422

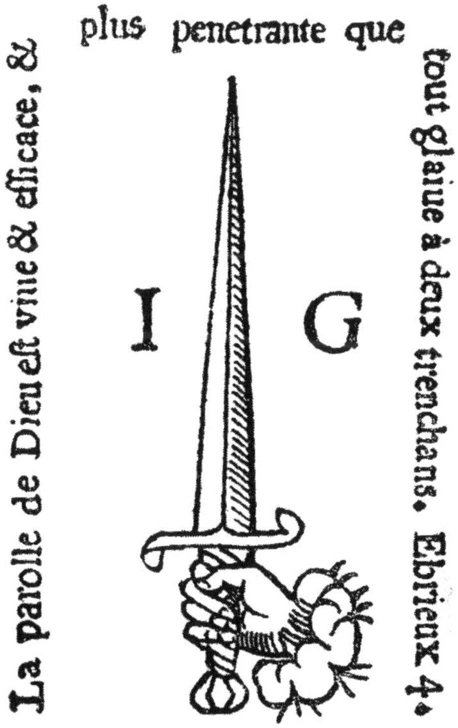
plus penetrante que
tout glaiue à deux trenchans. Ebrieux 4.
La parolle de Dieu est viue & efficace, &
I
G

423

SCTE·TRINITATIS

424

425

426

427

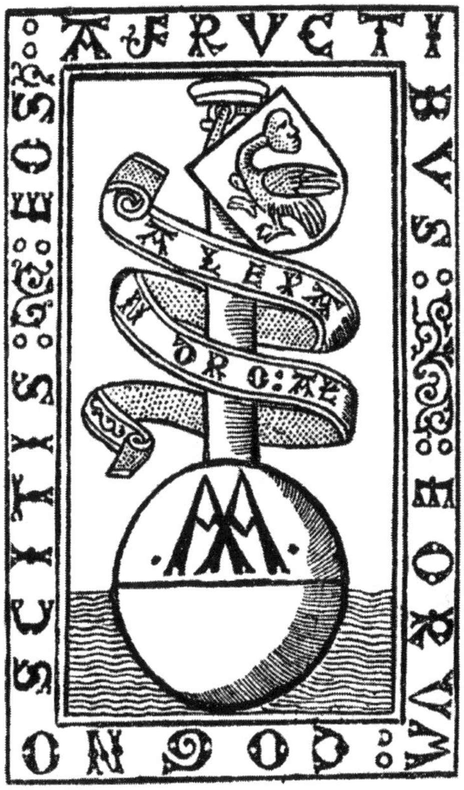

428

429

430

431

432

433

434

435

436

IEHAN BON HOMME.

437

INRI

438

439

APOC. XXI. EGO SITIENTI DABO DE FONTE AQVE VIVE GRATIS

440

441

PIETAS ET ALMA SCIENTIA· HASTA EST MEA, ET CLIPEVS MEVS

442

SCIENTIA
IMMVTA
BILIS.

443

444

IE HANTE
L'ARMONIE.

445

GIENS.OLIM
NVNC FV
PVGNABO.

446

447

TELLE · EST · LA · GLOIRE · DES · HOMMES
· I · D · P ·

448

INDOS CVRRIT
MERCATOR
AD

449

La coignée est ia mise à la racine des ar-
bres : parquoy , tout arbre qui ne fait
pas bō fruit, sera couppé & ietté au feu. Mat. III.

450

451

COËRCENDA
M
M
VOLVPTAS

452

453

LEARN MORE

At Vault Editions, our mission is to create the world's most diverse and comprehensive collection of image archives available for artists, designers and curious minds. If you have enjoyed this book, you can find more of our titles available at vaulteditions.com.

REVIEW THIS BOOK

As a small, family-owned independent publisher, reviews help spread the word about our work. We would be incredibly grateful if you could leave an honest review of this title wherever you purchased this book.

JOIN OUR COMMUNITY

Are you a creative and curious individual? If so, you will love our community on Instagram. Every day we share bizarre and beautiful artwork ranging from 17th and 18th-century natural history and scientific illustration, to mythical beasts, ornamental designs, anatomical illustration and more. Join our community of 100K+ people today—search @vault_editions on Instagram.

DOWNLOAD YOUR FILES

STEP ONE

Enter the following web address in your web browser on a desktop computer.

www.vaulteditions.com/vdi

STEP TWO

Enter the following unique password to access the download page:

vdi38572gbsdrx2

STEP THREE

Follow the prompts to access your high-resolution files.

TECHNICAL ASSISTANCE

For all technical assistance, please email: info@vaulteditions.com

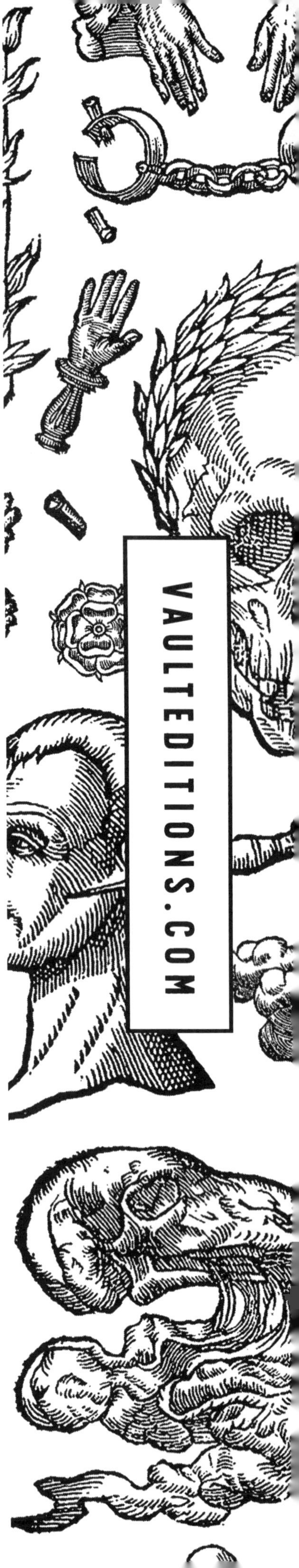

Made in the USA
Las Vegas, NV
11 September 2023

77436609R00062